Porsche Bella's Forever Home

Patricia A. Brill, PhD

Illustrated by Curt Walstead

Dedication

This book is dedicated to the teenage boy
who rescued Porsche Bella, along with her brother and sister;
and to the Lone Star Boxer Rescue Organization in
Houston, Texas for their tireless efforts to
find abandoned boxers a forever home.

Hello All—

　　Every rescue dog has a tale to tell. My tale is about my journey from being an abandoned pup left in the middle of a field to being adopted into a forever home.

　　I have learned that saving one dog will not change the world, but for me, my world was changed forever! I never knew how great life could be. I miss my brother and sister, but my new family was more than I could ever expect.

　　Every dog deserves a second chance. And what better way to give them a forever home than to adopt them.

　　I hope this book will encourage you to foster or adopt a dog today!

　　　　Love,

　　　　Porsche Bella

PORSCHE BELLA

As a lightning bolt crackled across the darkened sky, three white boxers huddled together next to a tree. "Why did they abandon us?" whined the little pup. "Why won't they come back for us?"

"Because we are white boxers," the brother replied. "Sometimes white boxers are blind or deaf when they are born so humans think we are imperfect. The breeder didn't want to keep us because he thought no one else would want us."

"I'm afraid," cried the little pup. "Don't worry," said the sister. "We'll stay close together tonight so we will be safe and warm."

The next morning the sister yelled. "Look! Someone is coming toward us!" It was a teenager. He called to them to come, but the three dogs started to run away. He called again and held up some food. Because the dogs were so hungry, they followed the boy to his home. The boy and his mother fostered the dogs until someone would adopt them.

Finally one day a man named Captain Zach and a woman named Dr. Pat came to meet the dogs. Because they already had four dogs living with them, they could only take one home so they chose the little pup.

As Dr. Pat approached to pick her up, the little pup ran behind her brother and sister and cried, "Please don't let them take me away from you. I will be sad without you!"

"Don't be sad," said the brother. "Although we will be apart, we will always have love for each other in our hearts."

Dr. Pat carried the little pup to the van. The pup was scared to get in. The last time the three dogs rode in a van they were dropped off in the middle of a field and no one ever came back for them.

But to the little pups' surprise, the van was filled with toys, puppy food, and a new designer doggie bed!

Finally after what seemed like a long ride, the little pup arrived at her new home. Afraid to go into the house, she stood in the middle of the garage shaking with fright. Suddenly four dogs gathered around her sniffing her from head to tail.

SNIF SNIF SNIF SNIF SNIF

The little pup cried out, "I'm scared, I feel all alone."

"Don't be scared," said Chevron. "You will never be alone again. This is your forever home."

"What is a forever home?" she asked.

"A forever home is where you will live happily ever after. You will never have to worry about being abandoned again. You will have new brothers and sisters, and all the treats you could ever possibly want."

"Treats? What are treats?" she asked.

"Don't worry," replied Chevron. "Turbo will teach you about treats."

"How do you know this will be my forever home? Our last owner dropped us off and never came back for us. For more than a week we waited for him to return to take us home. Night after night we huddled together to stay safe and warm. During the day we searched for food. We were so hungry our ribs stood out. How do you know I won't be abandoned again?" she asked.

"Because I too was abandoned," replied Chevron. "For months I lived behind a dumpster at a Chevron station. That's how I got my name. But one day Captain Zach and Dr. Pat rescued me. They put me into their car, and took me to their home. That was 15 years ago. Now that's a forever home."

"What about the other dogs in the house? Were they abandoned as well?"

"Yes" replied Chevron. "All of them were abandoned by their owners. But then they were rescued and adopted by Captain Zach and Dr. Pat. So now we all live in our forever home together."

"What are their names?" she asked.
"Turbo, Cayman, and Carrera."

"I don't have a name," she whimpered. "When the teenage boy found us we didn't have a collar with a nametag or a microchip. So no one knew who we were or where we lived."

"Not to worry," said Chevron. "I heard them say your name will be Porsche Bella."

"Porsche Bella," said the little pup. *"I like that name."*

"What if Turbo, Cayman, and Carrera won't like me?" she asked.

"They will like you if you follow our rules," said Chevron.

"I never had rules in my last home," said Porsche Bella. "What are your rules?"

"First, we must pray before each meal. We say:
Let's Pray.
Dear God,
Thank You for another day.

We get to run, and jump, and spin, and play.
We thank You for the food we are about to eat, our doggie beds, and all our treats.

We thank You for all the people You put in our lives, and we ask that You bless them in the way You know best.

And finally we pray for all the lost and abandoned dogs that they will be safe until they are found and adopted.
 Amen

Second. Never eat out of another dogs' food dish while they are eating, especially Cayman's. He will growl and snap at you.

Third, don't jump up on people when they come in the front door."

"Those are too many rules," sighed Porsche Bella.

Then she cried. "I miss my brother and sister. Why can't I be with them?"

"Because sometimes, brothers and sisters have to be separated before they are adopted. Not every person can take two or more dogs at one time. But I'm sure your brother and sister found a forever home just like you did!" said Chevron.

"Did I do something wrong to be abandoned?" asked Porsche Bella.

"NO!" said Chevron. "You didn't do anything wrong. People abandon dogs because they think it is the only possible solution. Sometimes situations change and people can't take care of animals any more. They might have died, lost their job, or moved to an apartment that doesn't allow pets."

As the weeks went by, Porsche Bella settled into her new forever home. One day as she was frolicking in the big back yard with her new brothers and sisters, she spun in the air and squealed, "I never knew how great life could be! I am so glad I got a second chance!"

Porsche Bella's Forever Home

© 2016 by Patricia A. Brill

Published by Functional Fitness L.L.C.

All rights reserved. No part of this book may be reproduced, stored, or transmitted by any mean (paperback)s--whether auditory, graphic, mechanical, or electronic—without written permission of the author, except for the inclusion of brief quotes in critical articles and reviews. Send inquiries to info@dogtalescollection.com.

ISBN: 978-0-9815551-9-5 (paperback)

Printed in America

Illustrated by Curt Walstead

Photo of Porsche Bella © 2015, Linda Lee Photography

Book design by DesignForBooks.com

www.ingramcontent.com/pod-product-compliance
Lightning Source LLC
Chambersburg PA
CBHW040731020526
44112CB00058B/2929